The fruit of the Spirit is...

The fruit
of the Spirit is...

J. V. Fesko

PUBLISHING WITH A MISSION

EP BOOKS
Faverdale North, Darlington, DL3 0PH, England

e-mail: sales@epbooks.org
web: http://www.epbooks.org

EP BOOKS USA
P. O. Box 614, Carlisle, PA 17013, USA

e-mail: usasales@epbooks.org
web: http://www.epbooks.us

First published 2011

British Library Cataloguing in Publication Data available

ISBN-13: 978-0-85234-736-2
ISBN-10: 0-85234-736-7

Printed and bound in Great Britain by
CPI Cox & Wyman, Reading, RG1 8EX

To my mother-in-law

Linda Riley Jones

Acknowledgements

I love the Old Testament. In fact, when I was in seminary, I first gave thought to pursuing graduate studies in the Old Testament. One of the things that really interests me is the connection between the testaments, especially the New Testament's use of the Old Testament. When I originally preached the substance of this book in a sermon series on Galatians, I was particularly enthralled with the Old Testament background to chapters five and six. I was always eager to share the material with others and taught it in a number of different settings: from the pulpit, the Sunday School lectern, and in my systematic theological courses at seminary. It was my wife, Anneke, who first suggested that I transform the material into book form. So, dear wife, I am grateful for your encouragement, support, and excellent suggestion. But I must also give thanks to David Woollin of EP Books who pursued the idea of publishing the work. David, I am grateful for all of your labours on my behalf. I am also grateful to the staff at EP Books for seeing this book through the publishing process.

I also want to mention the work of two scholars in particular that were of immense value for me in my study and preparation of this material: William Wilder's *Echoes of the Exodus Narrative in the Context and Background of Galatians 5:18*, and Greg Beale's *New Testament Commentary on the Use of the Old Testament*, and his article, 'The Old Testament Background of Paul's Reference to the "Fruit of the Spirit" in Galatians 5:22', *Bulletin for Biblical Research 15* (2005): 1-38. I found these resources to be immensely helpful and illuminating.

I dedicate this book to my mother-in-law, Linda Jones, who presently is in the midst of a great trial. My prayer for you, Mom, is that this book would be a source of encouragement and edification as you look to Christ and his Spirit to produce his holy fruit in you in the midst of this crucible of life.

My prayer is that many others will find the book personally edifying, and glorifying to our great covenant-keeping Lord. *Soli Deo Gloria*.

J. V. Fesko
January 2011
Escondido, California

Contents

Introduction

Godliness is a topic that brings about different reactions from different people. Some have a very negative view — stories like Nathaniel Hawthorne's *Scarlet Letter* come to mind, where people interested in moral purity relentlessly persecute a woman and her illegitimate child. For others, godliness is greatly desired because people feel burdened and weighed down by guilt, shame and sin. They desperately want to be freed from the sins that beset and hound them.

So then, what is godliness? Godliness is not simply an attitude of moral superiority but, rather, exhibiting the moral characteristics and qualities of God himself: righteousness, integrity, love, mercy, patience, wisdom, and the like. Godliness, therefore, is most certainly something that is to be desired. Paul once wrote to Timothy, and by extension the whole church: 'Train yourself for godliness,' (1 Timothy 4:7); and 'Pursue righteousness, godliness, faith, love, steadfastness, gentleness' (1 Timothy 6:11). Godliness is supposed to be one of the defining characteristics of God's people; it should not be viewed in a negative light. The portrait that Hawthorne paints in his *Scarlet Letter* represents a distortion of what true godliness is.

So if godliness is something that should mark God's people, the question naturally arises: How does one obtain it? How can a person become godly? Generally speaking, before a person can consider what he wants to become, he has to recognize who he is at present. In this case, it is absolutely fundamental that we first recognize our sinfulness and our utter inability to be godly. The Bible clearly spells out our sinfulness such as in Paul's letter to the Romans: 'All have turned aside; together they have become worthless; no one does good, not even one' (Rom. 3:12). Paul's statements were addressed to both Jew and Gentile alike, as he writes: 'For all have sinned and fall short of the glory of God' (Rom. 3:23). So we must first acknowledge our sinfulness. When we look into the mirror of the law and see its demands for moral perfection in our words, thoughts and deeds before both God and man, we must recognize how far we fall short. Even if we were able to claim a certain degree of fidelity to God's law, James gives us an important reminder that if we violate the law at one point, we are guilty of violating it all (James 2:10). Because we break the law and are held accountable for it all, we are therefore liable to its condemnation and curse. So as we travel down the road in the pursuit of godliness, the path of self-help and self-reformation is blocked by a massive obstacle — our sin and the law. But all is not lost.

We must give thanks to God in Christ because, as Paul writes to the Romans, for those who look to Christ by faith alone, which is ultimately a gift from God by the work of the Holy Spirit, there is no longer condemnation. Christ sets us free from the curse and condemnation of the law. He bore the curse of the law on our behalf and poured out his Holy Spirit upon us so that we would walk, not according to our former sinful ways, but according to the Spirit (Rom. 8:1-4). Godliness comes through faith in Christ through the work of the Holy Spirit — not through our own efforts to amass a stockpile of good works from which we can somehow improve our standing before God. In the words of Paul, may it never be! Rather, when a sinner looks to Christ by faith, the Holy Spirit produces godliness in him.

Another way Paul has described the work of the Spirit in producing godliness in the life of the believer is as the 'fruit' of the Spirit: love, joy, peace, patience, kindness, goodness, faithfulness, gentleness and self-control (Gal. 5:22-23). In other words, godliness is the fruit of the Spirit. Referring back to Paul's words to Timothy, he included godliness among the other virtues that he elsewhere identifies as the fruit of the Spirit (1 Tim. 6:11). In many ways, godliness is the term that best describes all of the fruit of the Spirit. Understanding what Paul has to say about the fruit of the Spirit can be immensely helpful to our growth in godliness. But all too often, when people read his famous statement, they see the different types of fruit that they should produce and so focus upon those characteristics to see if they can improve them. If a person struggles with a lack of patience, which leads to outbursts of anger and a loss of self-control, then he tries harder at being more patient. Perhaps some achieve a certain measure of success, but the real question is: What has the person accomplished? Has he merely done what any unbeliever might achieve through an anger management programme as he quietly mutters to himself, 'Serenity now, serenity now' in the face of trying circumstances? Or is the patience a manifestation of the work of Christ through the Spirit — the genuine fruit of the Spirit? Quite literally, there is a world of difference between a degree of patience that any unbeliever might produce, and the fruit of the Holy Spirit.

In order to understand the fruit of the Spirit and how they relate to the Christian, we must first understand the big picture. To that end, chapter one explains that big picture — how we arrived at the present state of affairs. We will see that God created the heavens and earth and placed Adam as his vicegerent over all of the earth and its creatures. Adam was a king and the earth was his kingdom. However, Adam forfeited his rule by rebelling against the authority of the sovereign King through his disobedience to the King's command. This necessitated God, the second person of the Trinity, the God-man, entering human history to redeem a people for himself and re-establish his kingdom. God would do this, as he did in the first creation, by making a new creation — a new heavens and earth. Just as in the first creation, God would create through the work of his Son and the Holy Spirit. God did not wait for the end of history to do this but begins the new heavens and earth in the middle of history through the work of Christ and the Spirit in the hearts and lives of believers.

Chapter two will look briefly at the greater context of Paul's epistle to the Galatians and then explore Galatians 5:16-18, which begins the apostle's explanation of the famous passage relating to the fruit of the Spirit. In order to gain a proper understanding of the fruit of the Spirit it is crucial to examine the Old Testament background to this holy fruit. Paul does not invent the idea of the fruit of the Spirit; he reaches back into Israel's history to its key formative event — the exodus from Egypt. Paul invokes the imagery of the pillar of fire by night and the cloud by day, an Old Testament manifestation of the Spirit, leading Israel on the exodus from Egypt. This event in Israel's past foreshadows how the Spirit now leads the people of God on the final exodus — an exodus not from under Pharaoh's rule, but from the tyranny of Satan, sin and death. Just as Israel of old walked in the Spirit, so Paul exhorts the Galatians to also walk in the Spirit. The Spirit, as Paul will show them, is the source of the fruit of godliness in their lives.

Chapter three shows how Paul taps into the ancient prophetic stream of Isaiah where God promised that he would send his Servant and the Spirit to bring forth fruitfulness throughout the creation. Paul not only digs into passages in the book of Isaiah that are evocative of the Genesis creation account, but he also draws upon Isaiah's use of the Old Testament exodus from Egypt. The images of the old creation and the Egyptian exodus foreshadow the new heavens and earth, and the final exodus. This exodus is not led by Moses but by one greater than Moses: Jesus; and the Holy Spirit. When Paul discusses the fruit of the Spirit he is, in effect, telling the Galatians that the long-awaited and promised blessings made by the prophet are now being fulfilled in them. The righteousness and holiness of the new heavens and earth had been inaugurated by Jesus through his life, death, resurrection, ascension, and his outpouring of the Spirit.

Chapter four explores what Paul has to say about the fruit of the Spirit. All too often we read worldly definitions into ideas like patience and love. Love becomes something that makes us feel good — warm and fuzzy. What we will see is that since the fruit of the Spirit is a result of the work of Christ, this is the manner by which Christ recreates fallen creatures in his image. Christ defines the fruit of the Spirit — if we want to know what love is, we must look to Christ. If we want to know what patience is, we must look to Christ. In so doing, we will see that Christ pours out his Spirit upon believers so that we will manifest his righteousness and godliness — and so be further conformed to Christ's image.

Chapter five addresses the question of how we can become godlier and manifest the fruit of the Spirit. All too often we believe that all we need to do is to try harder to be patient or more faithful. What we will see is that the only way that we can become godlier and manifest the fruit of the Spirit is by drawing near to Christ through his appointed means: word, sacrament and prayer.

So, then, before we proceed we need to ensure that we have an understanding of the big picture. We therefore must return to the beginning of all things and contemplate the history of two great kings, the first and last Adams.

1. The big picture:
the first and last Adams

A voice cried out, piercing the silent darkness, and said, 'Let there be light!' In less than a blink of an eye there was light. The King who had spoken these words had created a world and universe out of nothing and was now beginning to mould and shape the matter he had created. Like a brilliant architect and builder, the King separated the light from the darkness, and created lights to adorn the heavens. A beautiful array of lights inhabited the heavenly expanse that would illumine the earth below. The King created a glorious light to shine brilliantly and rule the day, and he created another light to rule the night. The sun and the moon would rule and were decked in glorious light.

But the King was not yet finished with his creation — there was still much to be done; and so he uttered another fiat in a kingly manner, and the creation responded — the Spirit of the King hovered over the miry chaotic waters and divided them in two. The King adorned his own throne with a sea of glass and created a mirror image of this picture in the earth below — the waters no longer covered the earth. Dry land emerged and the King called the waters below 'seas'. God saw the seas and filled them with all sorts of creatures of different shapes and sizes — some so small they were barely visible to the eye, and some so large that they seemed to dwarf all of the other creatures of the sea. The King looked out upon the heavens and filled the blue canvas with winged creatures of every kind. There were birds of every different colour and size. The creatures of the waters ruled the seas, and the birds of the sky ruled the heavens.

The King looked about the barren land and cried out yet again, 'Let the earth sprout vegetation, plants yielding seed, and fruit trees bearing fruit in which is their seed, each according to its kind, on the earth.' And the earth responded to the command of the King and burst forth with all sorts of grass, bushes, plants and trees, some of which were ornamented with dazzling fruit of all sorts of different colours — tantalizing reds, greens, oranges and yellows. God then filled the verdant earth with creatures — diminutive inch worms creeping along the ground, green lizards scampering about, cattle lowing in the fields, ferocious lions lurking about, and gargantuan elephants and giraffes ambulating about the plains. The King looked over all he had created and saw that everything was good. It was good because it reflected his wisdom and creativity, and was untainted and perfect in every way.

Yet there was still one last thing that the King wanted to do — he wanted to create a capstone, a crowning gem, to his creation. While the lights, the creatures of the seas, and the birds of the air each ruled their respective realms, the King wanted a creature to be invested with his own glory and image. He therefore created man, male and female, and invested them with his perfect, holy and righteous image. Not only did man have the perfect image of their Creator, but the King also gave them dominion over everything — the fish of the sea, the birds of the heavens, the animals of the field, indeed over the entire earth. The King gave his image to no other creature — man in all his perfection, glory and righteousness was inaugurated and installed as king over the earth. The King looked upon man and covenanted with him: 'Be fruitful and multiply and fill the earth and subdue it and have dominion over the fish of the sea and over the birds of the heavens and over every living thing that moves on the earth.' The creation rejoiced at the instalment of their king, a vicegerent for the King. The King looked over his creation, upon the capstone, his vicegerent, and pronounced it all 'very good'. The King then rested from all of his labours.

Not long after his instalment, the vicegerent laid down to rest — he laid down in a meadow, placed his hands behind his head, propped his head against a tree and looked out over his kingdom. He marvelled at its beauty and splendour and gave thanks to his King for all that had been given. A little while later, out of the corner of his eye, the vicegerent noticed a serpent, an intruder, enter the garden-temple that had been given as a special place where he and the King were to meet — where he was supposed to worship the King. Rather than swiftly dispatching the serpent, he curiously watched as it approached his wife and began to talk with her. Within earshot, the vicegerent listened to the conversation but chose not to act; instead he waited to see what his wife would do. The serpent hissed and told the woman that if they truly wanted to be like their King, they had to disregard the one prohibition they had been given — they had to consume the fruit of the one forbidden tree that was in the midst of the holy garden-temple. The serpent hissed that the King did not really tell them not to eat of the forbidden tree and that they would not die as the King had indicated. The curse of the covenant would not fall upon them as they had been warned, but they would become like the King himself, knowing good and evil. The woman looked upon the forbidden fruit, saw how delicious it looked, and perceived that it would indeed make them wise. So she took the fruit, placed it upon her lips, and bit down into its flesh. She then walked over to her husband and gave him some of the fruit, and he ate it too.

They then looked at one another in eager expectation; but instead discovered something else — they realized that they were both unclothed! They were horrified and grabbed the leaves of a nearby fig tree to sew together some makeshift clothing. When the King entered the garden-temple he called out to his vicegerent, but the man and the woman foolishly tried to hide themselves from his presence. They tried to hide themselves from the one who had created the cosmos, who spoke worlds into existence, who created the heights and the depths. The King saw through their foolish attempts and cursed them for their breach of the covenant. The man would now work by the sweat of his brow, and thorns and thistles would inhibit his labours. The woman had her pain in childbirth greatly increased and her desire would be for her husband's authority, and husbands would sinfully lord their authority over their wives. The King also cursed the serpent for his part in the breach of the King's covenant — the serpent would crawl upon his belly and eat the dust of the earth. Even though the King had every right to banish his rebellious vicegerent permanently, he showed mercy. The King promised that there would be another, a faithful vicegerent, the seed of the woman — he would crush the head of the serpent and the serpent would bruise his heel.

The man and woman were filled with hope and faith in the promise that the King had made. The man, Adam, renamed his wife. She was no longer *woman*; she was now, *Eve*, mother of all the living. The fallen vicegerent believed in the merciful promise that the King had made. But there were still great consequences to the vicegerent's rebellion. The King drove the fallen vicegerent from his presence, and out of the garden-temple, east of Eden. The fallen king also saw the kingdom that once belonged to him fall into the hands of the serpent. The prince of darkness was now the prince of the power of the air and the ruler of this age, an age that had now become evil because of Adam's rebellion. Not only did thorns and thistles hinder Adam's work, but thorns and thistles grew in the heart of man, in the heart of Adam's offspring. Though

Eve looked at the birth of their first child in the hope that it was the promised King in the flesh, the King who would crush the head of the serpent and restore the kingdom to fallen man, she and her husband were grieved to their core when their son killed his brother in anger. The fallen king could now only look over the corpse of his son and mourn that it was his breach of the covenant that brought all sorts of evil, wickedness and sin into his once pristine kingdom. And now a wicked and evil king sat upon the throne of this world. Adam could only look to the future in the hope of the promise of redemption that would come through the seed of the woman.

Adam's hope was fixed upon the promise of the gospel — the good news that the King, Yahweh, would come in the flesh to redeem a fallen people and restore his earthly kingdom. The people of God longed for the fulfilment of this promise and looked by faith to the coming King. In the fulness of time the God-man, the second person of the Trinity, came into the world in the middle of history — in the middle of the present evil age, an era ruled by the prince of the air. Jesus was welcomed as the King — his birth was heralded by the heavenly host, but something was very different about the reception of this King. Unlike Adam, one who was placed in a pristine world where the King provided every one of his needs, King Jesus was born and placed in a feeding trough for animals. The King of kings and Lord of lords, God in the flesh, entered the sinful world to redeem a people for himself. He would restore his Father's reign over the creation — he would cast out the ruler of this world.

When Jesus the King was tempted, Satan, the serpent of old, promised to give him all of the kingdoms of this world. Satan's temptations were filled with the same half-truths that he had told the man and the woman so long ago. Just as Satan told Adam and Eve that they would be like God if they ate of the fruit, Satan told Jesus that if he only made some bread out of stones, something to eat, if he only cast himself upon the rocks from a great height, or if he only bowed down to worship him, he would give him the place that Adam once held — he would give him the place as vicegerent. Jesus, however, saw through the lies. Jesus was obedient to the will of his Father, the King, and though he was equal with his Father, he did not consider his equality with him as something to be grasped or taken, like Adam tried to grasp the fruit of the tree in an attempt to gain equality with the King. Rather, he humbled himself and was obedient to his Father to the point of death, death on the cross. Because of his obedience, the King gave to Jesus the name that is above every name, the name at which every knee will bow and every tongue will confess, both in heaven and on earth, that Jesus is Lord, King over the entire cosmos, to the glory of God the Father.

In his life, death, resurrection and ascension to the right hand of the Father to rule over his enemies, Jesus secured the redemption of his people, those whom the Father has chosen. Those who look to Jesus by faith alone, which is a gift of the Holy Spirit, believe and are saved from the power of Satan, sin and death. They are no longer ruled by the despot, Satan. They are now under the reign and rule of the faithful vicegerent, Jesus. But Jesus did not come to save a people for himself, his royal subjects, to take them out of the world and float upon the clouds as disembodied spirits. Remember that when the King first created, he declared the creation 'good', even 'very good'. King Jesus, therefore, has come not only to save a people for himself, body and soul, but also to create once again — to create a new heavens and earth — a new creation that is even more beautiful and glorious than the first. Just as the King and his Holy Spirit created the first heavens and earth, so too now King Jesus creates the new heavens and earth in the midst of the old creation.

Like light shining in the darkness, King Jesus creates through the power of the gospel as the Holy Spirit applies it. By the preaching of the gospel, as people believe in him by faith alone, Jesus raises the dead to life. Not only does the Spirit, whom Jesus has sent, raise people from death to life, but he also creates in them his holy fruit — the fruit of the Spirit: love, joy, peace, patience, kindness, goodness, gentleness and self-control. This fruit is the antithesis of what characterizes the fallen kingdom of Adam, one that is marked by sin and wickedness — the works of the flesh: sexual immorality, impurity, sensuality, idolatry, sorcery, enmity, strife, jealousy, fits of anger, rivalries, dissensions, divisions, envy, drunkenness, orgies, and the like. In the midst of this sin-darkened kingdom, Jesus the faithful vicegerent and King creates anew and establishes his kingdom of light, where his royal subjects manifest this holy and righteous fruit. The big difference between the fallen kingdom of first Adam and the kingdom of Jesus, the last Adam, is that

Jesus' kingdom is eternal and unshakable. Nothing can overturn the rule of King Jesus because Jesus has definitively defeated the prince of this present evil age and at the consummation will crush his head as was prophesied so long ago.

As we have looked at the big picture, we have very quickly surveyed pre-redemptive and redemptive history, from Genesis to Revelation, the proton to the eschaton, the beginning to the end. With the big picture in view, we can now proceed and examine the specifics of how Jesus has poured out the Holy Spirit, and how the Spirit manifests his holy fruit in us. We will turn to Galatians and see how Paul begins to explain the life of godliness; but he does so evoking language from the Old Testament exodus from Egypt.

2. Walk by the Spirit

Read Galatians 5:16-18

Introduction

Galatians has historically been hailed as an epistle about the doctrine of justification by faith alone, and rightly so. Justification is an act of God where he pardons our sins and accepts us as perfectly righteous in his sight because by his free grace he accredits the perfect obedience of Christ to our account. But what many might not realize is that the epistle also deals with matters related to our sanctification, our growth in our conformity to the image of Christ, an image marked by godliness and righteousness. Paul emphasizes the truth of our justification by God's grace alone by faith alone in Christ alone in the opening chapters that lead up to chapter five. He has told the Galatians and the false teachers that they are not justified or saved by their obedience to the law but instead by looking to the work of Christ. Christ's *obedience* throughout the entirety of his life becomes our perfect obedience through faith alone. Christ's *death* becomes our death, suffering the penalty of the law, through faith alone. Christ's *resurrection* becomes ours and signals our own future resurrection from death — again, through faith alone. Our faith, we should note, is extraspective in nature — not introspective; we look outside of ourselves by faith alone to the life, death and resurrection of Christ for our salvation.

A typical response to the gospel, evident in Paul's letters, is that, if we are justified by faith alone, then who needs to be obedient? Should we not sin all the more so that we can receive greater amounts of God's grace? Paul's answer, of course, was a hearty, 'May it never be,' or, 'God forbid!' On the contrary, Paul explains that the Christian, whether Jew or Gentile, has been freed from the bondage of the law, not so that he can return to its slavery, but so that he can use his freedom to serve Christ — to use his members as instruments of righteousness and godliness (good works), not wickedness. Paul then addresses the importance of godliness and draws the reader's attention to the work of the Holy Spirit in our sanctification. As we proceed, however, I think it is crucial that we set aside our familiarity with the latter portion of chapter five. Too often, I believe, when we come to the famous passage on the fruit of the Spirit, we recite the list quickly, and then we move on. Instead, I hope to explain what Paul has written to help us better understand the instruction that he has given.

I believe that Paul has given us beautiful, profound, and biblically informed instruction. When I say 'biblically informed', I mean that he has the fabric of the Old Testament in the back of his mind as he writes. Specifically, it is the imagery of the Old Testament exodus that lies behind much of what Paul says, although there are other layers of Old Testament images that we will explore. Nevertheless, it is important to first recognize the Old Testament exodus as it echoes behind what Paul writes, as it will help us to understand not only what Paul is writing, but it will also help us in our own sanctification, our own growth in godliness. In other words, I want us to understand more clearly what Paul means when he says, 'walk by the Spirit'. In order to understand the fruit of the Spirit, we begin in Galatians 5:16-18 and will explore what Paul means when he writes that Christians are led by the Spirit and are not under the law.

Slavery and bondage under the law

Before we proceed, it is important that we first remind ourselves of the broader context of Paul's letter, particularly the way in which he has characterized life under the law. Recall the language that Paul has used to depict life under the law, or the Mosaic covenant: 'Now before faith came, we were held captive under the law, imprisoned until the coming faith would be revealed' (Gal. 3:23). Paul uses vivid imagery of captivity and imprisonment. Elsewhere Paul writes in a more specific manner, calling life under the law *slavery*: 'Formerly, when you did not know God, you were enslaved to those that by nature are not gods. But now that you have come to know God, or rather to be known by God, how can you turn back again to the weak and worthless elementary principles of the world, whose slaves you want to be once more?' (Gal. 4:8-9).

It may be appropriate at this point to ask *why* Paul characterizes life under the law, or the Mosaic covenant, as one of bondage and slavery. The evidence seems to indicate that Paul has in mind the Old Testament exodus and Israel's bondage and slavery to Pharaoh in Egypt. In the minds of a biblically informed first-century Jew, words such as slavery, bondage and captivity would invoke Israel's bondage in Egypt as Pharaoh's slaves. Moses came, however, and led Israel out of bondage into freedom. In the New Testament, it is not Moses who leads the people of God but rather Jesus Christ, one greater than Moses. As Paul explains in the previous chapter in Galatians, Christ was born under the law to redeem we who were under the law, so that, as Paul says, we might be adopted as God's sons (Gal. 4:5). Paul's point is that when a person looks to Christ by faith, he is freed from the bondage of the law and is justified in God's sight.

But notice what else happens to the believer: 'Christ redeemed us from the curse of the law by becoming a curse for us — for it is written, "Cursed is everyone who is hanged on a tree" — so that in Christ Jesus the blessing of Abraham might come to the Gentiles, so that we might receive the promised Spirit through faith' (Gal. 3:13-14). Coinciding with our justification by faith is the reception of the Holy Spirit. This complex of events, our redemption from the slavery and bondage of the law by the work of Christ, and our reception of the Holy Spirit, requires greater amplification against the background of the Old Testament exodus.

Old Testament exodus background

What happened during the Old Testament exodus and why would Paul have this event in the back of his mind as he explains the freedom that Christians have from the law? There are a number of instances in the books of the prophets which provide interesting information concerning the exodus. The LORD spoke through the prophet Haggai and told the Israelites: 'Work, for I am with you, declares the LORD of hosts, according to the covenant that I made with you when you came out of Egypt. My Spirit remains in your midst. Fear not' (Hag. 2:4b-5). God used the prophet to send a message of hope to the Israelites when they had returned to the promised land from the Babylonian exile, that he would remain in their midst. God reminded them that just as his Holy Spirit was with Israel during the exodus (remember the pillar of cloud by day and fire by night), so once again God would be in the midst of his people. He is making the point that God placed his Holy Spirit in Israel's midst throughout the time of their freedom from bondage and slavery in Egypt.

The prophet Isaiah also draws upon the exodus but goes into much greater detail than the prophet Haggai:

Then he remembered the days of old, of Moses and his people. Where is he who brought them up out of the sea with the shepherds of his flock? Where is he who put in the midst of them his Holy Spirit, who caused his glorious arm to go at the right hand of Moses, who divided the waters before them to make for himself an everlasting name, who led them through the depths? Like a horse in the desert, they did not stumble. Like livestock that go down into the valley, the Spirit of the LORD *gave them rest. So you led your people, to make for yourself a glorious name*

(Isa. 63:11-14).

The imagery the prophet uses is the LORD leading his people like a shepherd. But notice that Israel *walked* out of Egypt and followed the Spirit. Israel was led by the Spirit. The prophet Nehemiah uses the same Old Testament imagery when he describes the exodus:

The pillar of cloud to lead them in the way did not depart from them by day, nor the pillar of fire by night to light for them the way by which they should go. You gave your good Spirit to instruct them and did not withhold your manna from their mouth and gave them water for their thirst

(Neh. 9:19-20).

The psalmist, perhaps with the exodus in the back of his mind, calls upon the LORD: 'Teach me to do your will, for you are my God! Let your good Spirit lead me on level ground' (Ps. 143:10).

All of these passages paint a picture of God placing his Holy Spirit in the midst of his people during the exodus. Moreover, I believe these passages clearly point to the idea that it was the Spirit, represented by the cloud by day and by the pillar of fire by night, who led Israel out of bondage in Egypt and into freedom.

Returning to Galatians and Paul's instruction

When we consider this Old Testament background, as well as what Paul has stated thus far concerning the freedom from the slavery and bondage of the law, hopefully we can listen to Paul in a new light: 'But I say, walk by the Spirit, and you will not gratify the desires of the flesh' (Gal. 5:16). Why does Paul say 'walk by the Spirit'? Why not, 'live' or 'seek' the Spirit, for example? I believe Paul uses this phrase because the apostle has the collective imagery of the exodus in the back of his mind — God leading his people by the cloud and pillar of fire. In other words, the Old Testament foreshadows the redemption that would come through Christ. Christ, like Moses before but in a greater way, has liberated his people from the bondage and slavery of the law, and, like Israel of old, God's people must follow the Spirit on their pilgrimage to the promised land. We pilgrim, however, not to a piece of real estate in the Middle East, but to the New Jerusalem — to heaven itself.

So here, Paul is saying, we must follow the lead of the Holy Spirit, and if we do so, then we will not desire to satisfy and gratify the wicked desires of the flesh. Notice how Paul places the desires of the flesh in total antithesis to the desires of the Spirit: 'For the desires of the flesh are against the Spirit, and the desires of the Spirit are against the flesh, for these are opposed to each other, to keep you from doing the things you want to do' (Gal. 5:17). Here Paul shows us the totally contradictory nature of our former lives under the bondage and curse of the law versus our existence and life in Christ. In other words, we have been set free from the bondage of the law and we have been indwelled by the power of the Holy Spirit. We have not been freed so we can return to the bondage of the law. We have not been freed so we can use our Christ-wrought Spirit-applied freedom to sin. Or to put it in terms of the exodus narrative, we have not been freed from bondage in Egypt so we can return to that sweltering furnace of Pharaoh's cruel lordship.

Paul tells us that the desires of the flesh, which characterize life under the law, are opposed to the desires of the Spirit. Or we can state this antithesis in terms of the works of the flesh and the fruits of the Spirit. Sexual immorality, impurity, sensuality, idolatry, sorcery, enmity, strife, jealousy, fits of anger, rivalries, dissensions, divisions, envy, drunkenness and orgies are the complete and total opposite of love, joy, peace, patience, kindness, goodness, faithfulness, gentleness and self-control. We have been set free from the former and the curse of the law that justly falls upon us, and have been redeemed that the Spirit might inhabit us so that we produce the latter.

As we will see in the next chapter, quite literally the flesh and the Spirit are two ways that Paul refers to two entirely different and antithetical worlds. The former is the fallen kingdom and reign of the first Adam, the latter is the righteous reign and kingdom of the last Adam, Jesus Christ. The former is the old creation that is passing away, the latter is the new creation that has come and continues to unfold through the work of Christ and the Spirit. Paul is explaining in greater detail here in Galatians 5 something that he says more succinctly in other places: 'Therefore, if anyone is in Christ, he is a new creation. The old has passed away; behold, the new has come' (2 Cor. 5:17).

We need to keep in mind that Paul writes nothing new but instead draws upon Old Testament prophecies. For example, recall what Ezekiel prophesied concerning the work of the Spirit and the consequent godliness that would be manifest in believers: 'And I will give you a new heart, and a new spirit I will put within you. And I will remove the heart of stone from your flesh and give you a heart of flesh. And I will put my Spirit within you, and cause you to walk in my statutes and be careful to obey my rules' (Ezek. 36:26-27). Paul restates this same truth in a similar way, though once again with the backdrop of the exodus in view: 'And you show that you are a letter from Christ delivered by us, written not with ink but with the Spirit of the living God, not on tablets of stone but on tablets of human hearts' (2 Cor. 3:3). God gave Moses the law on tablets of stone, but now, under the final exodus led by Christ, God writes his law upon our hearts.

For all of these reasons, then, Paul can confidently tell the Galatians: 'But if you are led by the Spirit, you are not under the law' (Gal. 5:18). If the Spirit leads us, then we have the law of God written upon our hearts, and we have the indwelling power of God recreating us in the image of Christ, and enabling us to say 'no' to our sinful desires. Moreover, we are not under the bondage of the law — we are not subject to its curse because Christ bore the curse for us. We are not trapped under its demands for perfect obedience, because Christ has offered his perfect obedience on our behalf. Like Christ, who himself was led by the Spirit into the wilderness immediately after his baptism and was faithful when tested and tempted, we, who are united to Christ when we are tested, are indwelled by the Spirit and by faith have the ability to say 'no' to the temptations of sin.

Considering the implications

Everything that lies on and below the surface of these verses helps us to understand what Paul is saying in a deeper way so that his instruction can be of great benefit to our own growth in grace and godliness. Those who have been redeemed by Christ are marked by the indwelling power and presence of the Holy Spirit. This means that we are to be marked by righteousness and godliness, or more basically, that we are to be marked by good works! At the same time, I also hope that we have a greater understanding of our sanctification.

In other words, if Christ leads us on the final exodus by the Holy Spirit, as Old Testament Israel was led in the wilderness by the cloud by day and pillar of fire by night, then what can we learn from the exodus narratives that assist us in our own growth in grace? Recall that Israel was marked by complaint, rebellion, idolatry and sexual immorality. Paul describes the Israelite exodus:

> *I want you to know, brothers, that our fathers were all under the cloud, and all passed through the sea, and all were baptized into Moses in the cloud and in the sea, and all ate the same spiritual food, and all drank the same spiritual drink. For they drank from the spiritual Rock that followed them, and the Rock was Christ. Nevertheless, with most of them God was not pleased, for they were overthrown in the wilderness. Now these things took place as examples for us, that we might not desire evil as they did*

(1 Cor. 10:1-6).

We are just as prone to the sins that Old Testament Israel was, but at the same time we have an even greater resource at hand, namely the indwelling presence of the Holy Spirit.

Unlike Old Testament Israel who had the law written upon tablets of stone, we have the law written upon the tablets of our hearts. We also have the indwelling power of the Spirit enabling us to be obedient, even causing us to walk in God's statutes, to borrow Ezekiel's words. This hopefully alerts us to an important point that so many Christians miss

— namely, the nature of our sanctification. The law does not produce godliness. The law only condemns sin. Obedience does not produce godliness. Obedience that is carried out in the power of the flesh fails every time. Rather, only the Holy Spirit produces his fruit in us and enables us be obedient, to produce good works. In other words, in our sanctification, for our growth in godliness, we must seek the power of the Holy Spirit. The Spirit alone is both the source and the power of our sanctification, good works and obedience.

We must therefore seek the power of the Holy Spirit through God's appointed means: through the Word, preached, read and meditated upon; the sacraments, baptism and the Lord's Supper; and prayer. So often people cut themselves off from the means of grace: moving away from the church, failing to attend church, or even cutting themselves off from the sacraments. To do such things is to cut ourselves off from the power of the Holy Spirit. We will address these issues at greater length in the final chapter.

Conclusion

Christ has freed us from the despotic powers of Satan, sin and death, by his life, death, resurrection and ascension. Now, Jesus Christ, our great Shepherd, leads us through the wilderness on the last and final great exodus as Moses shepherded Israel of old. Christ, however, leads us by the presence of the Holy Spirit, just as Israel of old were led by the cloud by day and the pillar of fire by night. In our pilgrimage to the heavenly Jerusalem, we must follow the Holy Spirit. We are prone to wander and even at times try to return to the bondage from which we have been redeemed — to the very sin from which we have been delivered. Instead, if we walk by the Spirit, we will not gratify the desires of the flesh because if we are led by the Spirit, we are not under the law, its curse, slavery, or bondage. We have been set free by Christ through the work of his Spirit.

3. The fruit of the Spirit and the Old Testament

Read Galatians 5:19-25

Introduction

In the previous chapter we began to explore Paul's famous passage from Galatians on the fruit of the Spirit. We must continue to set aside our familiarity with what Paul has written and re-explore this famous passage with an eye to the Old Testament. Moving beyond a superficial understanding of basic moral qualities that Christians are supposed to manifest, instead, we should see how the characteristics that Paul attributes to Spirit-indwelt Christians run far deeper than that. Paul writes about the ongoing fulfilment of ancient prophecies promised long ago through the Old Testament.

Imagine that I were to give a lecture in a classroom in which I make references to the colour of the carpet and the walls without actually mentioning the specific colour. Then imagine that this lecture was deposited in a time capsule, buried, and opened two thousand years later. The reader would have no clue as to what colour the carpet and walls were — he could only hazard a guess; but he would never know for certain. But for all of those present, there would be no need to mention the colour of the walls and carpet because they would all see them before their very own eyes. This example hopefully illuminates the situation for Paul and the people of the Galatian churches, especially the Jews to whom Paul wrote.

Paul and his Jewish readers had a shared environment — the Old Testament. A first-century Jew who was well-versed in the Scriptures was intimately aware of many of the key Old Testament themes, terms, prophesies and promises. There would be no need for Paul to elaborate upon them. He could instead merely invoke these key ideas and terms and make an immediate connection with his readers. We had a glimpse of this reality previously as Paul used language that was evocative of Israel's Old Testament exodus to describe the Christian's freedom from the curse of the law.

In the previous chapter, Paul also used the exodus as his backdrop by characterizing life under the law as one of slavery, bondage, captivity and imprisonment, which was evocative of Israel's bondage in Egypt. On the other hand, Paul has characterized life in Christ as one of freedom, and one marked by the outpouring of the Spirit. We also saw Paul characterize the Christian life in terms of the exodus, specifically the idea of the Holy Spirit leading the Israelites through the wilderness in the cloud by day and the pillar of fire by night: 'But I say, walk by the Spirit, and you will not gratify the desires of the flesh... But if you are led by the Spirit, you are not under the law' (Gal. 5:16-18).

What we might not realize is that Paul continues this Old Testament theme of the final exodus in the verses that follow. What he does, however, is add layers of other Old Testament promises and prophesies, especially those promising a verdant, or fruitful, new creation. We must first, therefore, understand the Old Testament background to what Paul has written, and then consider the fruit of the Spirit against this backdrop. Hopefully, with this better understanding, we will be further equipped, as Paul has written elsewhere, for every good work.

Israel's unfruitfulness

We should pull back from Galatians 5 and look upon the grand picture of redemptive history and observe rebellious Israel. Isaiah prophesied of a coming exile in Babylon — an exile that was God's punishment for Israel's disobedience. In Isaiah 5 the prophet likens Israel to a vineyard on a fertile hill. Isaiah describes God's activities in planting the vineyard — God tilled the soil, cleared it of stones, and planted the choicest of vines. He built a watchtower, fashioned a wine vat and waited for the crop of grapes to grow so that he could make some wine. But the grapes that God planted yielded wild grapes, ones that could not be used to produce wine. What was God going to do to his wild grape-yielding vineyard? He would destroy it. God would remove its hedge, tear down its protective wall and allow the vineyard to be trampled. God would no longer tend it but allow weeds, thorns and thistles to grow in the vineyard; he would also seal the sky and let the vineyard wither under a drought — the sun would scorch it out of existence. The prophet then delivers this devastating blow: 'For the vineyard of the LORD of hosts is the house of Israel, and the men of Judah are his pleasant planting; and he looked for justice, but behold, bloodshed; for righteousness, but behold, an outcry!' (Isa. 5:7).

Within the world of Isaiah's parable, Israel was the unfruitful vineyard. The good grapes, or more generally, the fruit, that God desired to see grow was that of justice and righteousness. Take note, *righteousness* is one of the fruits of the Spirit. But instead of justice and righteousness Israel produced wild grapes — Israel produced bloodshed. Though Isaiah does not use Paul's specific terms for the works of the flesh, bloodshed is undoubtedly related to them. Was this the end for Israel? Would God have Israel taken into captivity and never rebuild his vineyard? Would the vineyard only be the haunt of wild beasts, thorns and thistles?

The coming fruitful servant and outpouring of the Spirit

In the following chapters Isaiah goes on to recount how God would show mercy to his people. Yes, God would carry his people into exile for their wickedness and rebellion, but he also promised through Isaiah that he would send his faithful and fruitful Servant to rebuild his vineyard. In Isaiah 11 God promised his people:

There shall come forth a shoot from the stump of Jesse, and a branch from his roots shall bear fruit. And the Spirit of the LORD shall rest upon him, the Spirit of wisdom and understanding, the Spirit of counsel and might, the Spirit of knowledge and the fear of the LORD. And his delight shall be in the fear of the LORD. He shall not judge by what his eyes see, or decide disputes by what his ears hear, but with righteousness he shall judge the poor, and decide with equity for the meek of the earth; and he shall strike the earth with the rod of his mouth, and with the breath of his lips he shall kill the wicked. Righteousness shall be the belt of his waist, and faithfulness the belt of his loins

(Isa. 11:1-5).

So often this passage is cited and read but perhaps people do not read it in context and see the connections between what has gone before in Isaiah 5 and unfruitful Israel. There may also be some who omit to draw any connection between Isaiah 11 and Galatians 5. But notice that the shoot from the root of Jesse would 'bear fruit'. This servant would be anointed with the Holy Spirit — note the connection between bearing fruit and the presence of the Spirit — and he would be filled with wisdom and knowledge, and would judge with righteousness, a fruit of the Spirit. But not only would he yield the righteousness that Israel failed to produce, but he would also wear *faithfulness* — another fruit of the Spirit — around his waist like a belt.

Later in Isaiah the prophet uses similar imagery to those found in Isaiah 11: 'In days to come Jacob shall take root, Israel shall blossom and put forth shoots and fill the whole world with fruit' (Isa. 27:6). The fruit of which Isaiah writes is not literal — Isaiah is not referring to bananas and mangos! Rather, he is referring to the fruit of righteousness and justice. And this fruit, or righteousness, would fill the whole earth! No longer would God confine righteousness to Israel alone but would see that his faithful Servant would spread this fruit throughout the entire creation.

In these passages God promises through the prophet that it is the shoot from the stump of Jesse, whom we all know is Jesus Christ, who will bear the fruit of righteousness. The Messiah will have the Spirit of the Lord rest upon him. The work of the Servant, Jesus, will bring fruit throughout the whole earth. The work of causing the earth to sprout with fruit, however, is not the work of the Servant alone. Isaiah returns to the imagery of God's vineyard later in his prophecy and writes:

> *For the palace is forsaken, the populous city deserted; the hill and the watchtower will become dens for ever, a joy of wild donkeys, a pasture of flocks; until the Spirit is poured upon us from on high, and the wilderness becomes a fruitful field, and the fruitful field is deemed a forest. Then justice will dwell in the wilderness, and righteousness abide in the fruitful field. And the*

effect of righteousness will be peace, and the result of
righteousness, quietness and trust for ever
(Isa. 32:14-17; cf. 44:2-4).

What Isaiah stated in somewhat general terms is now stated more specifically. God's vineyard would no longer be a haunt for wild animals, thistles and thorns, but would become a fruitful field with the outpouring of the Holy Spirit. Again notice the connection between the Spirit and fruit. But this time, Isaiah mentions another fruit of the Spirit, as he says that the effect of righteousness would be *peace*.

In effect, God told his people that his servant would come, as would the Spirit, and both would produce fruit throughout the creation — the fruit of righteousness, faithfulness and peace. Again, note that the fruit of which Isaiah writes is not literal, but is symbolic for righteousness and related virtues. If there is any doubt concerning this, hopefully the following clearly shows this point: 'Shower, O heavens, from above, and let the clouds rain down righteousness; let the earth open, that salvation and righteousness may bear fruit; let the earth cause them both to sprout; I the LORD have created it' (Isa. 45:8). God would open up the windows of heaven and send forth the rain to water the earth so that it could yield fruit; but the rain is symbolic language for the Holy Spirit and his work.

All of this imagery is undoubtedly creation-laden and echoes the opening chapters of Genesis, especially as Jesus Christ created the heavens and earth through the agency of the Holy Spirit. Recall that Paul says of Christ, 'For by him all things were created, in heaven and on earth' (Col. 1:16), and the Genesis account states: 'And the Spirit of God was hovering over the face of the waters' (Gen. 1:2). The creation was completed and ended with the first Adam standing in the midst of a host of fruit-bearing trees. It should be no surprise, then, how Isaiah characterizes Israel's renewal in the hands of the Spirit-anointed Servant of the Lord: 'For the LORD comforts Zion; he comforts all her waste places and makes her wilderness like Eden, her desert like the garden of the LORD; joy and gladness will be found in her, thanksgiving and the voice of song' (Isa. 51:3).

Let us summarize what we have seen thus far. God, through his Spirit-anointed fruit-bearing Servant, and through the outpouring of his Holy Spirit, will cause the earth to break forth in fruitfulness, and this fruitfulness is likened to the garden-temple of Eden. God will create a new heavens and earth by his Son and Spirit, and not only will it be verdant and fruitful, like the first creation, but it will be marked by righteousness and godliness. At the same time, this new creation imagery overlaps with that of the first and last exodus.

Returning to Galatians

When we return to Galatians we must keep this Old Testament background in mind — the exodus and the promised final exodus, the first creation and the promised new creation, and the promise of the Spirit-anointed fruit-bearing Servant of the Lord. We should also keep in mind the broader story of redemptive history. The first Adam was placed in the world to rule over it, to multiply God's image throughout the world, and to extend the garden-temple throughout the world. Adam failed — he rebelled against God and surrendered his reign to the powers of Satan, sin and death. The epoch or period of Adam is marked by the works of the flesh: 'Now the works of the flesh are evident: sexual immorality, impurity, sensuality, idolatry, sorcery, enmity, strife, jealousy, fits of anger, rivalries, dissensions, divisions, envy, drunkenness, orgies, and things like these' (Gal. 5:19-21). All of these things are the consequences of the sin of Adam, and all of those who are in Adam manifest these wicked works.

By way of contrast, notice how Paul characterizes our redemption by Christ. Jesus is one 'who gave himself for our sins to deliver us from the present evil age, according to the will of our God and Father' (Gal. 1:4). Jesus delivers us from the sin-dominated present evil age. When Christ delivers us, Paul explains: 'Christ redeemed us from the curse of the law by becoming a curse for us — for it is written, "Cursed is everyone who is hanged on a tree" — so that in Christ Jesus the blessing of Abraham might come to the Gentiles, so that we might receive the promised Spirit through faith' (Gal. 3:13-14). Here Paul writes of Isaiah's Servant who sends the fruit-bearing Spirit. Elsewhere in the New Testament we read of Christ's outpouring of the Spirit upon the church. Peter preached to the crowds at Pentecost: 'Being therefore exalted at the right hand of God, and having received from the

49

Father the promise of the Holy Spirit, he [Jesus] has poured out this that you yourselves are seeing and hearing' (Acts 2:33).

By this outpouring of the Spirit, the prophecies of Isaiah began to be fulfilled and the long-promised fruit that would ensue is manifest in those who are filled with the Holy Spirit: 'But the fruit of the Spirit is love, joy, peace, patience, kindness, goodness, faithfulness, gentleness, self-control; against such things there is no law' (Gal. 5:22-23). Quite literally, when we walk in the Spirit, the love that we show others, the joy that we know even during trials, the peace of God that we have and share with others through the gospel — in all of these things we are experiencing and manifesting the very things God promised through the prophet Isaiah over 2,500 years ago. Paul's famous fruit of the Spirit passage has a taproot that reaches down into the subterranean stream of the great Old Testament prophecies of Isaiah. What many do not realize, then, is that when they show love to another, God is fulfilling ancient promises of redemption through Christ and the Spirit in and through them.

There are two important points to note. First, notice what happens to those who unrepentantly exhibit the works of the flesh: 'I warn you, as I warned you before, that those who do such things will not inherit the kingdom of God' (Gal. 5:21). In other words, if a person does not repent of his sin and look to Christ by faith alone, he remains in the kingdom of Satan, the fallen reign of Adam. He remains a slave under the bondage of the law and therefore under its curse. By contrast, if we look to Christ by faith alone, then we inherit the kingdom of God, and it is Christ's kingdom, as we clearly see, that is marked by righteousness.

Second, notice the difference between Paul's use of the terms *works* of the flesh and the *fruit* of the Spirit. Why did Paul not call the fruit of the Spirit the *works* of the Spirit? I think Paul's choice of terms highlights the fact that ultimately it is the Spirit, as we rest in his power, who produces his fruit in us. We do not produce these characteristics of godliness, but rather Christ through his Spirit produces them in us. Think of Paul's famous statement taken from an earlier portion of Galatians: 'I have been crucified with Christ. It is no longer I who live, but Christ who lives in me. And the life I now live in the flesh I live by faith in the Son of God, who loved me and gave himself for me' (Gal. 2:20).

The false teachers were, through their own works, trying to produce the righteousness that God required. But in a stroke of genius, albeit an inspired stroke, Paul was showing the false teachers that they had failed to see how God had fulfilled the requirements of the law, not through greater efforts of the obedience of his people, but through his Son and the Spirit. Paul also makes this point when confronting a similar problem at the church in Rome: 'For God has done what the law, weakened by the flesh, could not do. By sending his own Son in the likeness of sinful flesh and for sin, he condemned sin in the flesh, in order that the righteous requirement of the law might be fulfilled in us, who walk not according to the flesh but according to the Spirit' (Rom. 8:3-4).

Exploring the implications

Given what Paul has written, what are the implications of all of this? Let me give a concrete example of these truths. When you respond to your children in patience, even though they have tested you and you have every right to be angry, the long-promised Spirit is producing his fruit in you. You resign your desire to respond in anger and instead rely upon the power of the Spirit to respond in patience. To act in such a manner is to walk in the Spirit; it is to pursue righteousness — to deny ourselves and follow Christ. So often, though, we choose the easy way in life. The works of the flesh are an easy path to walk. It is much easier to explode in a fit of anger and let everything out, dousing everyone around you in fire, rather than to deny yourself. Resorting to sinful anger is like trying to return to the fallen reign of Adam, or returning to Egypt even after the miraculous Red Sea deliverance.

How many of us have desired to do great and mighty things for the Lord with our lives? Yet, in our quest to do these great things, we neglect what Paul has written here. We think patience or gentleness are small and insignificant things. Does it really make a difference if I show my children, my neighbour, my co-worker, my spouse, or my extended family some patience? If we learn to see patience as the long-promised eschatological outpouring of the Spirit, that which fills the earth with the fruit of righteousness to the glory of God, how then might we answer that question?

Conclusion

I hope we see the works of the flesh for what they are — the last gasps of a fallen and corrupt kingdom that will come crashing down on the last day. I hope we see the fruit of the Spirit for what they are — the outpouring of the Spirit of Christ that enables and causes us to produce the fruit of righteousness to the glory of God our Father. In the next chapter, we will take a closer look at the works of the flesh and the fruit of the Spirit. But for now, it seems fitting to close this chapter with Paul's words: 'And those who belong to Christ Jesus have crucified the flesh with its passions and desires. If we live by the Spirit, let us also walk by the Spirit' (Gal. 5:24-25).

4. The fruit of the Spirit

Read Galatians 5:19-25

Introduction

In the previous chapter we explored Paul's famous 'fruit of the Spirit' passage against its Old Testament background, not only the exodus imagery, but also the prophetic promises of the outpouring of the Spirit, which resonated with creation imagery. We should briefly review these points for several reasons before we look more closely at the fruit of the Spirit.

First, we must recognize that these things have been promised from long ago. These events were foreshadowed in God's redemption of Israel from Egypt as he led his people on the exodus by the angel of the Lord and the glory-cloud (Exod. 14:19). Paul alludes to the Old Testament exodus when he exhorts the Galatians: 'But I say, walk by the Spirit, and you will not gratify the desires of the flesh … But if you are led by the Spirit, you are not under the law' (Gal. 5:16-18). The Lord led Israel like a shepherd leading his sheep. Not only were these realities of our salvation foreshadowed in Israel's exodus redemption, but they were promised long ago by the prophets, especially Isaiah: 'In days to come Jacob shall take root, Israel shall blossom and put forth shoots and fill the whole world with fruit' (Isa. 27:6). Again, Isaiah writes: 'Shower, O heavens, from above, and let the clouds rain down righteousness; let the earth open, that salvation and righteousness may bear fruit; let the earth cause them both to sprout; I the LORD have created it' (Isa. 45:8).

Second, when Paul places the works of the flesh in opposition to the fruit of the Spirit, he is contrasting two creations, two kingdoms — quite literally, two different worlds. The works of the flesh characterize the fallen reign of the first Adam, as he forfeited his reign to the powers of Satan, sin and death. The fruit of the Spirit characterizes the reign of the last Adam, Jesus Christ.

Third, we must realize that the fruit of the Spirit is not a new law. In other words, Paul is not placing new legal demands on God's people, 'You must be patient, kind, loving, etc, otherwise you will not inherit the kingdom of God.' No, perish the thought. Rather, the fruit of the Spirit is the work of Christ and of the Holy Spirit, not of man. Paul, for example, tells us that we are justified by grace alone through faith alone in Christ alone. But notice the consequence of our justification by faith alone: 'Christ redeemed us from the curse of the law by becoming a curse for us

— for it is written, "Cursed is everyone who is hanged on a tree" — so that in Christ Jesus the blessing of Abraham might come to the Gentiles, so that we might receive the promised Spirit through faith' (Gal. 3:13-14). Because we are declared righteous in God's sight, on account of the imputed righteousness of Christ, we receive the promised Holy Spirit — the indwelling power and presence of the fruit-producing Spirit.

Fourth, the righteousness that we see described in the fruit of the Spirit is first and foremost characteristic of Christ. We must not idealize these moral qualities in an abstract manner but rather define them in terms of God's revelation in Christ. By so doing, we hopefully realize that God is forming Christ in us, as we begin to see our need to reflect Christ's righteousness in every word, thought and deed.

Love, joy, peace

When we think of the first triad of characteristics, love, joy and peace, we know that these words have been defined in various different ways by the world. But within the context of the Scriptures there are unique definitions of them. To love is not to be filled with a warm fuzzy emotion, though I am sure at times it can involve such feelings. Rather, at the centre of love is sacrifice and selflessness. Christ's own love for us is manifest in that while we were God's enemies, Christ died for us. Love is one of the chief qualities that must mark God's people, which is manifest in a love for God (expressed through obedience) as well as a love for one another: 'By this we know that we love the children of God, when we love God and obey his commandments' (1 John 5:2). True love is set in total antithesis to the world's perversion of it — sexual immorality, orgies, idolatry, enmity and jealousy.

Likewise, joy is something that should mark us as the people of God. I think joy, however, can be confused with happiness. In other words, people hear that we should be filled with joy and laugh all the time. Make no mistake, joy should often be marked by laughter and excitement, but at the same time the Scriptures connect joy with other emotions. The author of the letter to the Hebrews describes Christ's crucifixion in terms of joy: 'Looking to Jesus, the founder and perfecter of our faith, who for the joy that was set before him endured the cross, despising the shame, and is seated at the right hand of the throne of God' (Heb. 12:2). Jesus was not clapping his hands as he giddily bore his cross. His suffering was, however, a time of joy for him. His joy was in knowing he was being obedient to his Father's will. I also suspect it was the knowledge that his suffering would produce life for his bride, the church, that gave him great joy. Christ had the joy of saving his people, but at the same time that joy was marked by suffering, and by death through crucifixion. There are times when God's people should be marked by great joy coupled with happiness and excitement, such as when a loved one makes a profession of faith in Christ. But at the same time, though perhaps not expressed with the same emotions, there can be a joy even in suffering. I have listened to saints suffering and dying from cancer tell me that it was a joy for them to serve the Lord and bring him glory even through the weakness caused by their illness. Such joy, of course, is often attended by great peace.

Peace, however, is something that the world lacks, whether it is the acrimony in an argument between people at work, arguments between a husband and wife, or with children, or violence in the world. The twentieth century was the bloodiest in history to date — the presence of war is certainly the absence of peace. Dissension, division, and even fits of anger can contribute to a lack of peace. In contrast to the ways of the world, the church is supposed to be marked by peace. How so? Well, our biggest problem prior to our conversion is that we have no peace with God — his wrath hangs over our heads like a sword suspended by a single strand of hair. But when God saves us, this enmity is destroyed: 'Therefore, since we have been justified by faith, we have peace with God through our Lord Jesus Christ' (Rom. 5:1). There is another dimension of peace, however, of which we should be aware.

Often people are marked by an absence of peace, and in its place we find anxiety or fear. The one who is indwelt by the Holy Spirit, because he knows the love of our heavenly Father given in Christ and applied by the Holy Spirit, because he knows that his all-provident hand provides for him with every need, and because he knows that Christ through the presence of the Spirit leads, guides and protects him, is filled with peace. In his letter to the Philippians, Paul writes about peace: 'Rejoice in the Lord always; again I will say, Rejoice. Let your reasonableness be known to everyone. The Lord is at hand; do not be anxious about anything, but in everything by prayer and supplication with thanksgiving let your requests be made known to God. And the peace of God, which surpasses all understanding, will guard your hearts and your minds in Christ Jesus' (Phil. 4:4-7).

Patience, kindness, goodness

Patience is linked, depending upon the situation, with love and peace, and even, arguably, joy as well. Patience is something that often does not at all mark the world. We live in a world where we have fast food, lunch in ten minutes or less, instant credit, and immediate results for a number of things. Patience is not something that we find all that frequently. I can remember as a child desperately wanting a new part for my bicycle, but I did not have enough money to pay for it. My parents could have easily paid for the part, but they wanted to teach me a helpful lesson about patience. I went to the cycle store and paid a deposit on the part. Then every few weeks I would go to the store and add a few more dollars towards its payment. I can remember finally being able to leave the store with the part in my hand! My parents taught me a good lesson about patience. Today, it seems far more likely that parents will simply pay for whatever their children want, knowing that instant gratification can be had with the swipe of a credit card.

Unlike the impatient world, patience is something that marks the people of God. We certainly see patience in Christ, who lovingly taught his disciples when they were slow to learn, listen and understand. I have often considered how a lesser man would have pulled out his hair, berated his disciples, and told them they were blockheads! Christ was patient. In such a manner we see a microcosm of God's patience in Christ's patience with his disciples. How long-suffering is the Lord with us, and yet how short-tempered are we with those around us? Often, patience is something that the church fails to exercise. We are impatient with those around us, wanting them to be at our own level of sanctification, or hold the same convictions that we do. If we recognize that our sanctification is ultimately the work of the Holy Spirit, then perhaps seeing an area where we think someone needs to be sanctified will be an opportunity to learn patience and the Holy Spirit will produce it in us.

By being patient with those around us we ultimately manifest the kindness and goodness of the Lord. Rather than sowing jealousy, strife, anger, envy, rivalries and the like, instead we must recognize that we are called to sow kindness and goodness in the church and beyond. Once again we know that the supreme manifestation of God's kindness and goodness to us has come in Christ through the Holy Spirit:

But when the goodness and loving kindness of God our Saviour appeared, he saved us, not because of works done by us in righteousness, but according to his own mercy, by the washing of regeneration and renewal of the Holy Spirit, whom he poured out on us richly through Jesus Christ our Saviour, so that being justified by his grace we might become heirs according to the hope of eternal life

(Titus 3:4-7).

If the Lord showed us kindness and goodness when we were his enemies, then as those indwelt by the Holy Spirit we must show kindness and goodness to others, even to our enemies. Rather than look for revenge, or respond in sarcasm or anger, our desire should be to respond in kindness and goodness — to show to others, especially those within the church, the love that we have received through Christ.

Faithfulness, gentleness, self-control

The Scriptures often closely link love and faithfulness together: 'Let not steadfast love and faithfulness forsake you; bind them round your neck; write them on the tablet of your heart' (Prov. 3:3). Proverbs insists upon this connection because steadfast love and faithfulness is something that marks the Lord: 'For your steadfast love is before my eyes, and I walk in your faithfulness' (Psa. 26:3). To be more specific, when we talk about the Lord I think we can identify faithfulness in terms of loyalty and commitment to his promises. This is why the Scriptures constantly celebrate the faithfulness of the Lord, because he has kept every one of his promises, and continues to do so. Faithfulness is ascribed to us in a similar way — in terms of loyalty, but also to our obedience and commitment to the Lord. God's people should be marked by faithfulness

— those who exhibit an obedience to the Lord's will. God's people should also be marked by a faithfulness, a loyalty, to the church. When so many things in life compete for our loyalty and faithfulness, it is Christ, our families, and the church that should top the list — all else is secondary.

Gentleness is related to self-control. So often the world is marked by harshness and cruelty. When proven right, are we interested in 'rubbing it in' and gloating? Do we treat others harshly, expecting them to 'toe the line' and then the moment they fail, do we ungraciously rebuke them? An illustration that comes to mind is the parable of the wicked servant. The servant sought the king's mercy for the great debt he owed and the king responded in gentleness. The servant, however, went out and demanded of his friend the relatively insignificant amount that was owed to him. Think over the entirety of your life and the many sins both small and great you have committed. Think of the law and its demand for perfect obedience. And then think of gentle ways in which the Lord has kindly dealt with you, not giving you what you deserve but instead pouring out his grace and mercy. While there are certainly times when Christians should respond in righteous anger, at the same time I believe the lion's share of the time our responses to the various situations in life call for gentleness. I think to respond in such a manner rather than give way to the anger or rage that might bubble in our hearts is a manifestation of self-control.

Self-control is not the idea of bottling up our anger until no one is watching and then letting it all out. Self-control is not biting our tongues whilst at the same time harbouring ill thoughts towards those around us. Self-control is not refraining from hitting someone and then pounding a punching bag or taking our aggression out at the gym by lifting weights. Rather, self-control is the ability to deny ourselves the indulgence of our sinful desires even when no one can see us, even when no one can know our thoughts. Self-control is ultimately the ability to be controlled, not by the sinful self, but by the Holy Spirit.

Conclusion

In all of these things we must see that God the Father, by the life, death, resurrection and ascension of Christ, applied by the Holy Spirit, is conforming us to the image of his Son. God breaks the power of Satan, sin and death by redeeming us from the kingdom of darkness, the fallen reign of Adam. He indwells us with his Holy Spirit and produces this fruit of righteousness in us. Unlike the curse of the law that hangs over the one who is under it, there is no such condemnation for those who are in Christ: 'And those who belong to Christ Jesus have crucified the flesh with its passions and desires' (Gal. 5:24). Like Israel leaving the furnace of Egypt behind, Christ liberates us from the tyranny of Satan, sin and death — our sinful nature is put to death with its passions and desires. Once freed from the power of Satan, sin and death, we must seek the power of the Holy Spirit so that he continues to produce this fruit in us: 'If we live by the Spirit, let us also walk by the Spirit' (Gal. 5:25). As we reflect upon this passage, we need to realize that only Christ through his Spirit enables us to manifest the fruit of the Spirit. We cannot produce this fruit on our own. Our chief desire should be that this fruit of righteousness, and not the works of the flesh, would be evident in us. We should pray that we would be so marked that we would edify the body of Christ, love our neighbour, and bring glory to our triune Lord.

5. Drawing near to Christ

Introduction

Now that we have a better understanding of the fruit of the Spirit, the question undoubtedly arises: How do I obtain this fruit? In one sense, this question has been touched upon throughout the book thus far. We must never forget that godliness and the fruit of the Spirit cannot be found within ourselves. Rather, we must look to Christ by faith alone, which is a gift of the Holy Spirit, and trust in his life, death, resurrection and ascension on our behalf to save us from our sins. Only Christ's life of perfect obedience can fulfil the law's demands for sinless perfection. Only Christ's sinless sacrifice upon the cross can fulfil the law's demands for the curse against the one who violates the law. Only Christ's resurrection from the dead breaks the bond of sin and death and prophetically declares our own resurrection from the dead on the last day. And only Christ's ascension to the right hand of the Father from where he poured out the Holy Spirit upon the church can yield the fruit of godliness and righteousness in our lives. Our redemption, pure and simple, is a work of Christ and the Spirit from beginning to end; he is both the author and finisher of our salvation.

But at the same time, we must realize that Christ and the Spirit employ means to bring about our redemption. The means of Christ's appointment are his Word, the sacraments (baptism and the Lord's Supper) and prayer. We will briefly explore each of these means so that we understand how Christ employs them and enables us through the work of the Spirit to draw near to Christ. But we will also briefly explore the use of the means of grace in the face of struggles and trials. In drawing near to Christ we are then further conformed to his holy image and the Spirit produces his fruit of godliness and righteousness in us.

The Word of God

When we read the opening chapters of the Bible we can ascertain the power of the Word quite easily — God spoke worlds into existence out of nothing. The same all-powerful word that God spoke in the beginning is the same power he wields in our salvation. Paul writes: 'For God, who said, "Let light shine out of darkness," has shone in our hearts to give the light of the knowledge of the glory of God in the face of Jesus

Christ' (2 Cor. 4:6). Paul elsewhere tells us that the gospel is the power of God for salvation (Rom. 1:16-17). The apostle confidently tells us that the Word is breathed out by God and is useful for teaching, reproof, training in righteousness, and for equipping the saints for every good work (2 Tim. 3:16-17). The Word of God is definitely powerful, and is the means by which he wields the saving power of the gospel upon sinners in desperate need of redemption. This means that when we desire to draw near to Christ and be further conformed to his holy image, we can do so through the reading of the Word. When we read the Bible, we listen intently with our minds to Christ speaking to us, and the Holy Spirit applies the Word to our lives so that we yield his holy fruit. When we read the law, for example, the Spirit uses it to convict us of our sin and causes us to flee to Christ, our only hope, for redemption, salvation, and even our growth in godliness.

But what we may not realize is that the Word of God is especially powerful when it is preached in the midst of the gathered body of Christ, the church. The Word is beneficial to us when we read it seeking greater conformity to Christ's image, but God has specifically called and gifted certain men with the ability to preach and teach the Word of God to the church. In Paul's letter to the Ephesians the apostle explains that in the wake of the ascension of Christ to the right hand of the Father, Christ has poured out the Spirit upon the church, and the Spirit has dispensed his gifts to the church: 'And he gave some, apostles; and some, prophets; and some, evangelists; and some, pastors and teachers; for the perfecting of the saints, for the work of the ministry, for the edifying of the body of Christ' (Eph. 4:11-12, KJV). The Spirit gave apostles and prophets to the early church so that they could give to the church the New Testament Scriptures. The apostles and prophets, Paul tells us, are part of the foundation of the church, which has Christ as the chief cornerstone (Eph. 2:20). With the death of the New Testament apostles and prophets, the task of propagating the Word of God has been passed on to evangelists, pastors and teachers. But take note, these men exercise their gift of evangelizing, preaching, or teaching, to the specific end of edifying, or building up, the church. When ministers of the gospel faithfully preach the Word of God and focus upon the person and work of Christ, the same power that brought worlds into existence is unleashed upon the people of God in corporate worship. Like Moses who struck the rock to bring forth water in a dry desert land, preachers bring forth the life-giving, Spirit-empowered Word of God that purges us of our sin and conforms us to the holy image of Christ.

All too often when it comes to the Word of God, people are spiritual bulimics and anorexics. They either completely avoid the Word altogether (anorexia), or they will feast upon the Word and then purge themselves of it (bulimia). Then people wonder why they are spiritually weak, beset by habitual sin, and struggling in their growth in grace, godliness and righteousness. If we truly desire to be conformed to the image of Christ and see the fruit of the Spirit manifest in our lives, we must draw near to Christ through the

Word of God. We must write his Word upon the walls of our hearts, meditate upon it night and day, and dutifully attend to the preaching of the Word by not forsaking the weekly dominical gathering of the saints in corporate worship (Heb. 10:25).

The sacraments

Beyond a shadow of a doubt, God has spoken to his people in his Word — we can hear his voice when we read aloud the words written in ink on the pages of our Bibles. However, God has not only spoken to us with ink and paper, but he has also spoken to us with water, bread and wine. Throughout redemptive history God has employed signs and seals for the covenant oath bonds that he has made with his people. Consider, for example, God's covenant with Abraham — that he would bless him with an heir from Abraham's very own body and would give to him descendants as numerous as the stars in the heavens (Gen. 15:1-6). God not only spoke those words to Abraham, which were subsequently inscripturated, but he also gave to Abraham a sign and seal of that verbal covenant promise — circumcision. Circumcision is the visible word — it was a visible sign of God's verbal covenantal promise to Abraham. The same can be said about baptism. Baptism visibly preaches the gospel of Jesus Christ, our death, burial and resurrection with Christ that we receive through faith alone and the indwelling power and presence of the Holy Spirit. Likewise, the Lord's Supper visibly preaches the gospel of Christ —

his body broken and his blood shed for us, that which brings us forgiveness, redemption and holiness. God never intended that baptism and the Lord's Supper should function by themselves, but rather as signs and seals of the verbal and now written promises of the gospel.

So when a preacher heralds the gospel of Christ and administers the Lord's Supper — the visible word — he is visibly preaching the gospel that has just been proclaimed. God uses Word and sacrament to preach not merely to our minds and hearts, but to all of our senses. We hear the Word of God with our ears and we see the Word of God with our eyes when we observe a baptism. We feel the Word of God when we receive the water of baptism. And we can even say that we taste and smell the Word of God when we partake of the bread and the wine. In effect, God preaches the gospel to all of our senses, which is a reminder that we will be wholly redeemed, body and soul.

The sad truth is that people do not realize the importance of the sacraments for a healthy spiritual diet. All too often the sacraments are relegated to the museum of 'traditional worship', something that people no longer need. Another common occurrence is that people think that when a person is being baptized, the only one benefiting from the sacrament is the one baptized; the rest of the congregation is a gallery of spectators. In other settings, the Lord's Supper is not celebrated with a great degree of frequency, whether out of neglect or because it is deemed too special to be observed more than once or twice a year. If we recognize that when the sacraments are coupled to the preaching of the Word, they are the means by which Christ conforms us to his image when they are applied to God's people. Christ's invisible Word goes out through the preaching of the Word and his visible word goes forth through baptism and the Lord's Supper. When we watch a baptism, we are not mere spectators but watch with our eyes the proclamation of the gospel. When we consume the bread and drink the wine, we touch the visible words of the gospel with our senses: taste, touch and smell. As we watch with our eyes or touch with our hands, our minds are drawn to the verbal promises of God's Word which have been preached and proclaimed, and through this the Spirit employs both Word and sacrament in our growth in grace. The sacraments help us, therefore, to seek Christ and his Spirit to grow in grace, godliness and righteousness — to manifest the fruit of the Spirit.

Prayer

Beyond Word and sacrament, the third element of a healthy spiritual diet is prayer. The apostle Paul explains in his epistle to the Romans that prayer is unique, in that the Holy Spirit intercedes on our behalf in prayer. When we draw near to Christ through prayer and find ourselves at a loss for words, not knowing how or what to pray, the Spirit carries our needs to the heavenly holy of holies, to the throne of Christ. Paul writes: 'Likewise the Spirit helps us in our weakness. For we do not know what to pray for as we ought, but the Spirit himself intercedes for us with groanings too deep for words. And he who searches hearts knows what is the mind of the Spirit, because the Spirit intercedes for the saints according to the will of God' (Rom. 8:26-27). Prayer, then, is the opportunity to enter into the presence of God through the mediation of Christ, our great High Priest, and through the intercession of the Holy Spirit, and cry out to our triune God for his assistance in our struggle with sin. Through prayer, we not only give thanks to God for all he has done for us, and praise him for who he is, but we also seek the strength of the Holy Spirit in our growth in grace.

Prayer in many ways is the school of Christ — it is the place where we learn to die to ourselves, our sinful desires, where we learn to say with our hearts and minds, 'Not my will, but yours, be done' (Luke 22:42). Far too many Christians fail to pray and know little to nothing of the power of prayer. When we struggle with sin, we must pray that God would give to us greater faith, a hunger and thirst for his Word, and a greater desire for godliness — that we would decrease and Christ would increase. Prayer is vital if we desire to draw near to Christ, make progress in our sanctification, and manifest the fruit of the Spirit.

Drawing near to Christ in the midst of struggle and trial

There are often times in the life of the believer that are marked by struggle and trial. These times can make a person feel as though he is spiritually stagnant or even regressing in his spiritual growth. What is a person to do in the face of persistent sin when it seems as though he cannot overcome his problems? What is a person to do if he faces doubt, perhaps even doubting the certainty of his salvation or of Christ's promises? What is a person to do when it seems as though his world is crashing around him and that God has forgotten his promises to save and sanctify his people?

The first thing we must realize is that we are not the first people in redemptive history to face struggles, doubts and trials. Think of John the Baptist. John was the one person out of billions of people in history who was chosen by God to be the personal herald of the Messiah. John alone was privileged to cry out, 'Behold, the Lamb of God, who takes away the sin of the world!' (John 1:29) and then personally baptize the Son of God. John was undoubtedly filled with hope and excitement, but then was filled with questions and confusion. John expected Jesus to judge the hypocrites and the wicked, but instead John was thrown in prison. In the face of his doubts, John sent some of his disciples to seek Christ and ask him whether he was the long-awaited Messiah. Jesus told John's disciples to tell him: 'The blind receive their sight and the lame walk, lepers are cleansed and the deaf hear, and the dead are raised up, and the poor have good news preached to them' (Matt. 11:5). Christ pointed John to his own messianic work. In effect, Christ told John, 'Look to me by faith.'

In the Old Testament the prophet Habakkuk was quite perplexed by what he saw happening to Israel. The prophet was dismayed because he saw the wicked pagan nation of Babylon attacking and destroying Israel, God's people. The prophet asked quite pointedly: 'You who are of purer eyes than to see evil and cannot look at wrong, why do you idly look at traitors and are silent when the wicked swallows up the man more righteous than he?' (Hab. 1:13). God responded to Habakkuk's complaint: 'The righteous shall live by his faith' (Hab. 2:4b). In the midst of the chaos and the apparent injustice, God was calling the righteous to trust him — to believe in him and the promised redemption that would come through the Messiah by faith.

Think of Paul's famous 'thorn in the flesh'. We do not know the precise nature of Paul's thorn. Was it someone or a group of people who persecuted him? Was it a physical ailment? Was it a time of trial or struggle? Regardless of the nature of the thorn, we know that Paul was desperate to be freed from it. He pleaded with the Lord three times to remove it, but God's response to Paul was: 'My grace is sufficient for you, for my power is made perfect in weakness' (2 Cor. 12:9).

What we must realize is that though God through Christ and the Spirit has given us his fruit, this does not mean that we will be free from struggles with sin, doubts, fears, or trials. In fact, it is more likely that as we mature in the faith we will find that our struggles *increase*. Why? When we ask to be conformed to the image of Christ and to bear the fruit of the Spirit, we should not be surprised when God gives us the opportunity to exercise those Spirit-given gifts. What good is patience if we do not exercise it? What good is love if we do not, especially in the face of hatred and anger, show it to others? How are we to grow in our faith unless we are challenged, brought to the end of ourselves, and cry out to Christ for his grace? It is often the case that the trials and struggles of life are the crucible in which God conforms us to the holy image of his Son. The trials and struggles with sin are like the smelter's fire where the Lord refines and purifies us, removing the dross of sin so that holiness and purity remain.

When we face such circumstances, our response should not be one of retreat and withdrawal. Rather, it is in the midst of these challenging circumstances in life that we must pursue Christ through his appointed means all the more. When we find ourselves starving and in need of nourishment, should we flee *from* the Lord or flee *to* him, that we might feed upon him, the true manna from heaven? When we are desperately thirsty, should we flee into the desert or seek shelter in the oasis of Christ and drink from the water that he offers, the water that permanently quenches our thirst, the water of eternal life? To return to the exodus motif, as we pilgrim to the promised land, the New Jerusalem, as we walk in the Spirit, we must feed upon the manna from heaven, Jesus Christ, so we have strength for the journey. We must drink from the rock, Jesus Christ, so we are not thirsty in a dry desert land.

Conclusion

We have only touched briefly upon the means by which we can draw near to Christ — Word, sacrament and prayer. If our desire is to manifest the fruit of the Spirit, then we must diligently attend to the means that Christ has appointed for our salvation. Inherent in our use of these means is an implicit acknowledgement that we are incapable of producing the fruit of the Spirit on our own. In looking to the Word by faith, whether by reading or hearing it preached, we acknowledge that only Christ through the Spirit saves and sanctifies. By hearing the Word and seeing the visible words of God in baptism and the Lord's Supper, God preaches to our senses, 'Christ saves you, delivers you from the miry depths of death, washes and cleanses you, and raises you to walk in the newness of life. Christ has lived a perfect life of obedience in fulfilment of every jot and tittle of the law but nevertheless had his body broken in death and shed his blood in payment of the debt you owed, and now eagerly await the consummation of all things when Christ will gather you with the rest of the church from the four corners of the earth to feast at the marriage supper of the Lamb!' In prayer, we cry out to our triune God, 'Save me! Sanctify me! Manifest the fruit of the Spirit in me!' If we truly desire to manifest the fruit of the Spirit, the in-breaking of heaven on earth, the long-ago prophesied blessings, we must draw near to Christ. We can only draw near to Christ through his appointed means — Word, sacrament and prayer.

Conclusion

Every Christian should desire to manifest godliness and the fruit of the Spirit. Good intentions and our own efforts to pull ourselves up by our moral bootstraps, while commendable, will always fall short of the godliness and righteousness of Christ. The only way that we can grow in godliness and manifest the fruit of the Spirit is by seeking Christ by faith alone through Word, sacrament and prayer. As we mediate upon what Paul has written about the fruit, we will see that God's promises have preceded our own desires for godliness and therefore undergird and give us hope knowing that he is faithful to redeem, save and keep his word. God has begun to create a new heavens and earth in the midst of this sin-darkened world. He has done so through the work of his Son and the Spirit as believers manifest the holy fruit of righteousness — fruit that will one day fill the entire earth. For the present, like Israel of old, we must walk in the Spirit; and by so doing we will not gratify the desires of the flesh, but instead manifest love, joy, peace, patience, kindness, goodness, gentleness, faithfulness and self-control. Rest in the work of Christ, and recognize that it is no longer you who lives but Christ who lives in you. One day, all of God's people will cross the threshold of the celestial city, the New Jerusalem, and never struggle with the desire to return to Egypt, to the bondage of the law. Until that day, seek Christ in the visible and invisible word, Word and sacrament, and cry out in prayer that Christ would conform us to his holy and righteous image.